ULTIMATE MACHINES

Motorbikes

Rob Colson

PowerKiDS
press

New York

Published in 2013 by The Rosen Publishing Group, Inc.
29 East 21st Street, New York, NY 10010

Senior Editor: Julia Adams
Produced by Tall Tree Ltd
Editor, Tall Tree: Jon Richards
Designer: Ben Ruocco

Photo Credits: 1 Michael Stokes/Shutterstock.com, 2 Harley Davidson, 4 Philip Lange /Shutterstock.com, 5t Drew Macdonald/Dreamstime.com, 5b Shotsstudio/Dreamstime.com, 6 BMW AG, 7t BMW AG, 7b BMW AG, 8 Harley Davidson, 9t Joachim Köhler/GNU Sharealike, 9b Aleksandr Stikhin/Dreamstime.com, 10 Łukasz Jaskowiak | Dreamstime.com, 11t Radzinski/GNU, 11b Peter Brauns/Dreamstime.com, 12 Yamaha, 13t Khafizov Ivan Harisovich/Shutterstock.com, 13b B.Stefanov/Shutterstock.com, 14 Phillip W Hubbard/ Shutterstock.com, 14–15 Terry Poche/Shutterstock.com, 15t Michael Stokes/Shutterstock.com, 16 Honda, 17t Honda, 17b Biker Biker/GNU, 18 Yamaha, 19t BMW AG, 19b MorePixels/istockphoto, 20 Yamaha, 21t Yamaha, 21b azaphoto/Shutterstock.com, 24 Terry Poche/Shutterstock.com

Library of Congress Cataloging-in-Publication Data

Colson, Rob, 1971–
Motorbikes / by Rob Colson.
     p. cm. — (Ultimate machines)
Includes index.
ISBN 978-1-4777-0066-2 (library binding) — ISBN 978-1-4777-0117-1 (pbk.) —
ISBN 978-1-4777-0118-8 (6-pack)
1. Motorcycles—Juvenile literature. I. Title.
TL440.15.C65 2013
629.227'5—dc23

2012021179

Manufactured in the United States of America

CPSIA Compliance Information: Batch #W13PK6: For Further Information contact Rosen Publishing, New York, New York at 1-800-237-9932

Contents

Wheel Power

Motorcycles come in many different shapes and sizes, from tiny scooters to enormous drag bikes. What they all have in common is two wheels and an engine.

There are about 200 million motorbikes in the world, making them one of the most popular forms of motorized transport. In competitions, motorbike riders race each other or perform daring tricks.

These riders are competing in a sidecar speedway race. The passenger shifts his or her weight from side to side to keep the bike balanced around corners.

Amazing design

A motorbike can carry a passenger by attaching a sidecar. The sidecar has one wheel, so this turns the bike into a three-wheeled vehicle. Sidecars were very popular in the 1950s, when most people did not own cars. Today, it is much more common to see passengers sitting on the bike behind the rider.

Road racing

Motorbikes can be raced on specially built tracks or on roads that have been closed to the public. The most famous road race of all is the Isle of Man TT, which is held every year on the roads of the Isle of Man. It is a time trial, which means that each rider is timed over a set number of laps of a circuit. The rider with the fastest time wins the race.

The Isle of Man TT has been held for more than 100 years. Thousands of fans flock to the island every year to watch the racing.

The very first motorbike was made by German inventors Gottlieb Daimler and Wilhelm Maybach in 1885. This replica of their bike is on display in the Mercedes-Benz museum in Stuttgart, Germany.

Superbikes

Many kinds of bike are raced around tracks and superbikes are some of the fastest. They are based on the design of motorbikes that you see on the road.

Superbikes have the same shape and engine as road bikes, while other parts have been altered. The gears are changed to provide faster acceleration, and the bikes have special electronics systems to give more power from the engine.

British rider James Toseland has twice won the World Superbike Championship. Here he tests out a BMW S 1000 RR.

Taking corners

Superbike riders lean over when they go around a corner. This allows them to take the corner at higher speeds. Footrests and exhausts are placed higher up than other road bikes, such as cruisers and tourers. This means that they do not scrape along the ground as the riders lean over.

Superbike riders lean over so much that their knees touch the ground. They wear tough padding to protect their knees from injury.

TECHNICAL DATA

BMW S 1000 RR

YEARS OF PRODUCTION
2010–present
ENGINE SIZE **999 cc**
NUMBER OF CYLINDERS **4**
GEARBOX **6-speed**
FRONT WHEEL TRAVEL **4.7 inches (120 mm)**
REAR WHEEL TRAVEL **5.1 inches (130 mm)**
WEIGHT **860 pounds (390 kg)**
FUEL CAPACITY **4.6 gallons (17.5 L)**
TOP SPEED **over 125 miles per hour (200 km/h)**

Amazing design

Superbikes are designed to be aerodynamic, which means that they cut through the air easily. A specially designed shell, called a fairing, is placed over the frame. The shape of the fairing allows air to flow smoothly around the bike. It also directs some of the air over the engine to keep it cool. To make the fairings the very best shape, motorcycle designers test them in wind tunnels. They study the results on computers.

Superbike riders crouch low over their bikes to make the most aerodynamic shape possible.

Cruisers

Harley Davidson is probably the most famous manufacturer of motorbikes in the world. They make a kind of motorbike called a cruiser.

Unlike a racing bike, on which the rider leans forward, the rider of a cruiser sits in an upright position. Harley Davidsons are large cruisers with loud, rumbling engines. You are likely to hear one coming before you see it!

The V-Rod VRSCAW is a powerful cruiser with a long body inspired by the design of drag bikes (see pages 14–15).

Customizing

Harley Davidson owners often turn their motorbikes into custom bikes. This means that they have changed the bike's size and shape to make it unique. Many owners make the forks longer so that the front wheel sticks out. Others fit their bike with wider handlebars or a bigger gas tank.

This customized Harley Davidson is fitted with extra-long exhausts and front forks as well as wide handlebars. It is a replica of one that was used in the movie Easy Rider.

Ridges on the cylinders called cooling fins help to stop the cylinders from getting too hot. The fins make a large surface area for cooling air to pass over.

Amazing design

A motorbike's engine contains cylinders. Inside the cylinders, pistons pump up and down to make the power that turns the wheels. On a Harley Davidson, the engine's cylinders are arranged in pairs in a "V" shape. This arrangement allows the engine to produce lots of power at low revolutions per minute (rpm). The Harley Davidson's low rpm gives it the distinctive "rumble" sound.

TECHNICAL DATA

V-Rod VRSCAW

YEARS OF PRODUCTION **2007–2010**
ENGINE SIZE **1,250 cc**
NUMBER OF CYLINDERS **4**
GEARBOX **5-speed**
FRONT WHEEL TRAVEL **4 inches (100 mm)**
REAR WHEEL TRAVEL **4 inches (100 mm)**
WEIGHT **670 pounds (304 kg)**
FUEL CAPACITY **5.3 gallons (20 L)**
TOP SPEED **over 125 miles per hour (200 km/h)**

Speedway

The bikes used in speedway racing are very different from road bikes. They have only one gear and no brakes. Their engines run on a fuel called methanol, which is a form of alcohol.

These bikes are designed for races that take place on an oval-shaped dirt track. Between four and six riders compete in races over four laps of the track.

Speedway races are fast and furious. A race lasts about 1 minute, and the lead changes many times. The bikes reach speeds of up to 70 miles per hour (110 km/h) on straightaways.

Amazing design

A speedway track is covered with small stones and pieces of dirt to allow the riders to slide around corners (see below). To stop the dirt and stones from being thrown up by the bikes and injuring other riders, all speedway bikes are fitted with dirt deflectors. These pieces of shatterproof plastic are attached behind the rear wheels.

TECHNICAL DATA

Jawa 889
YEARS OF PRODUCTION
1999–present
ENGINE SIZE **500 cc**
NUMBER OF CYLINDERS **1**
GEARBOX **1 gear**
FRONT WHEEL TRAVEL **adjustable**
REAR WHEEL TRAVEL **no rear suspension**
WEIGHT **175 pounds (80 kg)**
FUEL CAPACITY
less than 0.3 gallons (1 L) of methanol
TOP SPEED **70 miles per hour
(110 km/h)**

Broadsiding

As speedway bikes have no brakes, riders use a special technique called broadsiding to take the bends in a race. The rear wheel skids, and the rider turns the handlebars in the opposite direction to the turn. The front wheel points in the direction the rider wants to go, while the rear wheel slides out to one side.

Speedway races are always held in an counterclockwise direction. This means that the riders only make left turns. The exhaust is placed on the right where it will not be damaged during turns.

Motocross

Racing motorbikes over cross-country courses is called motocross. Motocross bikes are designed to be strong but lightweight and flexible.

To reduce weight, the frame of a motocross bike is made from light but strong aluminum. The tires have deep grooves to grip the muddy ground.

swingarm attaches wheel to shock absorbers

front forks

Amazing design

Motocross bikes need to be fitted with good suspension to absorb bumps on the track. At the front, the forks that connect the handlebars to the front wheel slide in and out to absorb the force. The rear wheel is fitted with shock absorbers. Riders change the suspension to suit the course. Hard suspension gives a faster flat speed. Soft suspension is better for extremely bumpy courses.

TECHNICAL DATA

Yamaha YZ450F

YEARS OF PRODUCTION **2010–present**

ENGINE SIZE **450 cc**

NUMBER OF CYLINDERS **1**

GEARBOX **5-speed**

FRONT WHEEL TRAVEL **12 inches (310 mm)**

REAR WHEEL TRAVEL **12.3 inches (310 mm)**

WEIGHT (WITH FULL TANK) **247 pounds (112 kg)**

FUEL CAPACITY **1.6 gallons (6 L)**

TOP SPEED **93 miles per hour (150 km/h)**

Dirt-track racing

Motocross races take place on purpose-built dirt tracks. Riders race each other over a set number of laps of the track. Tracks are built to give riders plenty of challenges. Track designers will build up piles of dirt to form ramps from which the riders can take off high into the air. The outside edge of the track's corners are built up into slopes called berms. These allow riders to take the corners at higher speeds, making for more exciting races.

A rider takes a high jump in a motocross race. While jumps are an exciting part of the race, riders will try not to go too high or they will lose speed.

Drag Bikes

The biggest and fastest motorbikes are drag bikes. Some drag bikes are heavily modified road bikes, but the fastest are completely custom-built.

Drag bikes compete in drag races along a straight track. The bikes do not have to turn corners, so they are designed to go as fast as possible in a straight line.

The fastest drag bike in the world is ridden by US rider Larry McBride (left). He is nicknamed "Spiderman" because of the way he lies on top of his bike. McBride holds the world record over a 1,320 foot (402 m) track of 5.7 seconds.

Amazing design

Drag bikes are designed so that the rider crouches down very low to create an aerodynamic shape. On the fastest drag bikes the rider may even be lying flat on top of the fuel tank and engine! Drag bikes accelerate very quickly, causing the front wheel to lift off the ground. Long bars at the back stop the bikes from rising up into a dangerous wheelie.

Blink and you miss it

In drag races, two riders race head-to-head along a track that is 1,320 feet (402 m) long. From a stationary start, the bikes reach 62 miles per hour (100 km/h) in less than a second. By the time they cross the finish line, they are traveling at over 190 miles per hour (300 km/h). Races last between six and nine seconds, depending on the class.

Drag bikes are divided into different classes, depending on how powerful they are. The fastest class is called "Top Fuel."

TECHNICAL DATA

Larry McBride's drag bike

YEARS OF PRODUCTION
made in 1994

ENGINE SIZE **1,511 cc**

GEARBOX **2 gear**

BODY **Carbon fiber**

WEIGHT **1,030 pounds (467 kg)**

FUEL CAPACITY
6 gallons (23 L) of nitromethane

FUEL USED PER RACE
4.2 gallons (16 L)

TOP SPEED
250 miles per hour (400 km/h)

Tourers

Touring motorbikes, or tourers, are large, powerful bikes. They are designed to give a comfortable ride on long-distance journeys.

The bikes have large fairings and windscreens to protect the rider in bad weather, and large fuel tanks so that they can ride farther between fill-ups. As on cruisers, the rider sits in an upright position.

The Honda Goldwing is a full-dress tourer. This means that it has very large fairings for protection and built-in saddlebags for luggage.

An LCD display on the dashboard of the Goldwing shows the rider all kinds of information about the bike's performance.

Amazing design

Modern tourers, such as the Goldwing, are fitted with many features designed to make the ride safer and more comfortable. The Goldwing has GPS satellite navigation, heated handlebars and seats, and even a music system. It is also fitted with an air bag, which blows up from under the dashboard to protect the rider in a crash.

The six cylinders in the Goldwing's engine are in a "flat-six" arrangement. This means that they are placed horizontally in two rows of three. The flat-six arrangement gives the bike a low center of gravity, which makes it more balanced and stable.

Reverse gear

The engines in large touring motorcycles are as big and powerful as the engine of a family-sized car. This makes the bikes very heavy. It is hard to wheel them backward without the help of the engine. Unusual for a motorbike, the Goldwing overcomes this problem with a reverse gear.

TECHNICAL DATA

Goldwing GL1800

YEARS OF PRODUCTION
2001–present
ENGINE SIZE **1,800 cc**
NUMBER OF CYLINDERS **6**
GEARBOX **5 gears**
FRONT WHEEL TRAVEL **5.5 inches (140 mm)**
REAR WHEEL TRAVEL **4 inches (100 mm)**
WEIGHT **920 pounds (417 kg)**
FUEL CAPACITY **6.6 gallons (25 L)**
TOP SPEED **over 125 miles per hour (200 km/h)**

Scooters

Small motorbikes with a platform for the rider's feet to rest on are called scooters. Scooters are small bikes designed for riding around city streets.

Scooters are cheap to buy, and are very popular in parts of the world where people cannot afford cars, or where parking a car is difficult.

A scooter's small engine is not attached to the frame of the bike. Instead, it moves with the rear wheel.

TECHNICAL DATA

Yamaha Zuma (pictured left)

YEARS OF PRODUCTION **2011–present**

ENGINE SIZE **49 cc**

NUMBER OF CYLINDERS **1**

GEARBOX **Automatic**

FRONT WHEEL TRAVEL **2.6 inches (66 mm)**

REAR WHEEL TRAVEL **2.4 inches (60 mm)**

WEIGHT **207 pounds (94 kg)**

FUEL CAPACITY **1.5 gallons (5.7 L)**

TOP SPEED **42 miles per hour (68 km/h)**

Like the driver of a car, the rider in a BMW C1-E is safely strapped in using seatbelts.

Amazing design

The BMW C1-E scooter is not powered by gas but by electricity. The C1-E is designed to be as safe as a car. The frame of the scooter is shaped to protect the rider in the event of a crash. The C1-E is not yet available for sale, but BMW thinks that in the future, motorcycles in cities will all look like this.

The Wasp

The most famous make of scooter is the Vespa. "Vespa" is the Italian word for "wasp." The scooter gets its name because its handlebars stick out like the antennae of an insect. The first Vespas were made in Italy in 1946. They became fashionable across the world after one was seen zooming around the streets of Rome in the 1953 film *Roman Holiday*.

The Vespa is instantly recognizable with its distinctive wide front fairing.

The Air Tricker

The Air Tricker is an experimental model made by Japanese company Yamaha. It is designed for commuting and also for doing simple tricks.

The frame of the Air Tricker is very similar to the frame of a mountain bike. The handlebars can turn a full 360 degrees, which is very useful for performing tricks.

The Air Tricker has pegs at the center of the rear and front wheels. Skilled trick riders stand on the pegs to perform advanced tricks such as the spins, just as BMX riders do.

Amazing design

A light bike is essential when you want to perform tricks. The Air Tricker's body is made from a special material called carbon fiber, which is very strong, but lighter than metal. This design makes the Air Tricker 44 pounds (20 kg) lighter than supermoto bikes, which are lightweight bikes designed for off-road racing and stunts. Because the Air Tricker is so light, riders are able to perform tricks that would be impossible on any other type of motorbike.

A trick rider performs an endo on a supermoto bike, a trick in which the rider tips the bike forward and balances on the front wheel.

TECHNICAL DATA

Air Tricker

YEARS OF PRODUCTION
not yet in production
ENGINE SIZE **250 cc**
NUMBER OF CYLINDERS **1**
GEARBOX **5 gears**
FRONT WHEEL TRAVEL **7.1 inches (180 mm)**
REAR WHEEL TRAVEL **6.8 inches (172 mm)**
WEIGHT **192 pounds (87 kg)**
FUEL CAPACITY **1.6 gallons (6 L)**
TOP SPEED **not yet tested**

Concept bike

Yamaha developed the Air Tricker as a concept bike. This means that it is not yet available in stores. A concept bike is a new design that can be seen by the public at motor shows. If the company believes it will be popular, the new model goes into production.

Glossary

aerodynamic (er-oh-dy-NA-mik)
Shaped to reduce air resistance when moving at high speed.

air resistance (EHR rih-ZIS-tens) The force caused by air pushing back against an object that is moving.

center of gravity (SEN-tur UV GRA-vih-tee) The place within an object where its weight is balanced. A bike with a low center of gravity is harder to push over.

customize (KUS-tuh-myz) To change parts of a bike bought in a shop in order to give it a unique look or to alter the power of the bike.

cylinder (SIH-len-der) A chamber in an engine inside which a piston pumps up and down.

experimental (ek-sper-uh-MEN-tul) Designed to test new ideas. Manufacturers may make experimental models to test new technology and see how well it works. They may also want to find out how popular the idea is with the public.

fairing (FAYR-ing) A shell placed over the frame of a motorbike to give it a more aerodynamic shape or to protect the rider.

gears (GEERZ) A system of cogs that transfers power from the engine to the wheels. Low gears give extra power for acceleration. High gears are used for faster speeds.

Global Positioning System (GPS) (GLOH-bul puh-ZIH-shun-ing SIS-tum) A system that uses satellites to figure out where a person is at any given moment.

ramp (RAMP) A piece of track where one end is higher than the other. Ramps are used by motorcycle riders to perform jumps.

replica (REH-plih-kuh) A copy of an original design that tries to be as close to the original as possible.

speedway (SPEED-way) A type of motorbike racing where riders race around an oval track that is covered with small stones and dirt.

suspension (suh-SPENT-shun) A system of springs and shock absorbers that makes the ride smoother as the wheels pass over bumps or as a rider lands a jump.

tread (TRED) The part of a tire that makes contact with the ground. The tread of a tire has a pattern of grooves in it to improve the tire's grip.

wind tunnel (WIND TUH-nel) A chamber in which air is passed at high speed over models. By studying the way the air passes over objects in wind tunnels, designers can figure out the most efficient shapes for their designs.

Models at a Glance

Model	Years in Production	Top Speed	Did You Know?
BMW S 1000 R	2010–present	over 125 miles per hour (200 km/h)	At least 1,000 road models have to be sold so that a bike can qualify for the Superbike World Championship.
Harley Davidson V-Rod VRSCAW	2007–2010	over 125 miles per hour (200 km/h)	Harley Davidson bikes are called "hogs" after a pig that was the mascot of their racing team in the 1920s.
Jawa 889	in production	68 miles per hour (110 km/h)	As the bikes do not have brakes, speed-way riders will often lay the bikes down on the track to stop.
Yamaha YZ450F	2010–present	93 miles per hour (150 km/h)	As well as motorbikes, the Yamaha Corporation makes boats, golf carts, and even musical instruments.
Goldwing GL1800	2001–present	over 125 miles per hour (200 km/h)	Goldwings are now full-dress tourers, but the first models in 1974 were sold without any fairings.
Yamaha Zuma	2011–present	30 miles per hour (48 km/h)	Zumas are limited to a top speed of 30 miles per hour (48 km/h). They can reach 37 miles per hour (60 km/h), but that speed is considered dangerous.
Yamaha Air Tricker	not yet in production	not yet tested	Yamaha is developing a new electric bike with two engines—one on each wheel.

Websites

Due to the changing nature of Internet links, PowerKids Press has developed an online list of websites related to the subject of this book. This site is updated regularly. Please use this link to access the list:

www.powerkidslinks.com/ulma/motor/

Index